IMAGES OF WAR

GERMAN HALF-TRACKS AT WAR 1939–1945

RARE PHOTOGRAPHS FROM WARTIME ARCHIVES

Paul Thomas

Pen & Sword
MILITARY

First published in Great Britain in 2012
and reprinted in this format in 2017 by
PEN & SWORD MILITARY
An imprint of
Pen & Sword Books Ltd
Yorkshire - Philadelphia

Copyright © Paul Thomas, 2012, 2017

ISBN 978 1 84884 482 7

The right of Paul Thomas to be identified as Author of this work has been asserted by him in accordance with the Copyright, Designs and Patents Act 1988.

A CIP catalogue record for this book is available from the British Library.

All rights reserved. No part of this book may be reproduced, transmitted, downloaded, decompiled or reverse engineered in any form or by any means, electronic or mechanical including photocopying, recording or by any information storage and retrieval system, without permission from the Publisher in writing. NO AI TRAINING: Without in any way limiting the Author's and Publisher's exclusive rights under copyright, any use of this publication to "train" generative artificial intelligence (AI) technologies to generate text is expressly prohibited. The Author and Publisher reserve all rights to license uses of this work for generative AI training and development of machine learning language models.

Typeset by Concept, Huddersfield, West Yorkshire HD4 5JL
Printed and bound in the UK by CPI Group (UK) Ltd, Croydon, CR0 4YY.

The Publisher's authorised representative in the EU for product safety is Authorised Rep Compliance Ltd., Ground Floor, 71 Lower Baggot Street, Dublin D02 P593, Ireland. | www.arccompliance.com

For a complete list of Pen & Sword titles please contact

PEN & SWORD BOOKS LIMITED
47 Church Street, Barnsley, South Yorkshire, S70 2AS, England
E-mail: enquiries@pen-and-sword.co.uk
Website: www.pen-and-sword.co.uk

or

PEN AND SWORD BOOKS
1950 Lawrence Road, Havertown, PA 19083, USA
E-mail: uspen-and-sword@casematepublishers.com
Website: www.penandswordbooks.com

Contents

Introduction **4**

Chapter One
   Early Years of Victory **5**

Chapter Two
   1941 .... **29**

Chapter Three
   1942 .... **52**

Chapter Four
   1943 .... **74**

Chapter Five
   1944 .... **95**

Chapter Six
   1945 .... **111**

Appendix
   Artillery Prime Movers **121**

Introduction

The performance of the German Army on the battlefield was attributed mainly to one vehicle that transported troops, ordnance and supplies to the front. It was called the half-track. These front-wheel steering vehicles with tracked drive transformed the fighting ability of both the *Wehrmacht* and *Waffen-SS* during the Second World War. This book reveals the complete illustrated history of the half-track and shows just how versatile these vehicles were in combat. Various half-tracks were built during the war, and production of the Sd.Kfz.251 variant, for instance, saw over 16,000 of them pour off the production line between 1940 and late 1944.

The book analyzes the development of the half-track and shows its increased role in combat, where newer variants were given main armaments in order to increase the overall firepower on the battlefield and support the advancing troops and Panzers to the front lines.

The full range of Hitler's half-tracks is covered in this book, ranging from the Sd.Kfz.10, Sdk.Kfz.7/1 self-propelled flak gun, Sd.Kfz6 and Sd.Kfz.8 prime mover, to the most popular half-track of them all, the Sd.Kfz.251 medium infantry armoured vehicle. Despite being lightly armoured, the Sd.Kfz.251 could maintain a relatively modest speed and manoeuvre across country and keep up with the fast moving armoured spearheads.

German Half-tracks at War is a captivating glimpse of these formidable machines, and will undoubtedly be of great interest to military historians as well as modellers and war-gamers.

Chapter One

Early Years of Victory

The invasion of Poland was the first time that the half-track was used extensively on the battlefield. Whilst the bulk of the *Wehrmacht* was still animal draught in 1939, there were only a few hundred vehicles that were half-track to tow ordnance, carry troops and supplies to the battlefront.

Spearheading one of the first promising attacks into Poland on 1 September 1939 was Army Group North, under the command of General Günther Hans von Kluge's Fourth Army. Kluge controlled five infantry divisions, plus two motorized divisions and the Third Panzer Division under General Heinz Guderian. The main thrust of the Fourth Army was east and south, sealing off and then destroying General Bortnowski's Pomorze Army, which was situated in what was known as the Polish corridor. All main efforts were carried out by the army's XIX Corps, under the faithful command of the Panzer ace, General Heinz Guderian. Bearing the brunt of this German armoured stampede stood the Pomorze Army, which consisted of five infantry divisions and one cavalry brigade. Throughout the first day of intensive fighting, Kluge's army caused such severe losses to the Pomorze Army that it was forced to reluctantly withdraw in total confusion.

Further east, separated by the Polish corridor in East Prussia, General Georg von Kuechler's Third Army made a number of thrusting all-out attacks south from the Prussian border in the direction of Warsaw against the Polish Narew Group and Modlin Army. Under Kuechler's command were seven advanced infantry divisions, an *ad hoc* panzer division consisting of SS-Panzer Division '*Kempf*', which incorporated SS-Panzer Regiment Deutschland, and four brigade-size commands, all of which were divided under three corps.

To the south, German forces were inflicting almost equal misery upon the enemy. Army Group South's main task was to try and engage the enemy as far forward of the Vistula and eliminate any attempt he might make to retreat east behind the line of the Vistula and San. It was for this reason that the Southern Army Group were ordered to reach the Vistula and San with the greatest possible speed.

Over the next few days both the German Northern and Southern groups continued to make furious thrusts on all fronts. As this great advance gathered momentum, more towns and villages fell to the onrushing forces. The campaign had taken on the character that was to remain for the few weeks that followed. Everywhere north, south and east, the fronts were shrinking, cracking slowly but surely under the massive German pressure. In this unparalleled armoured dash, some units had covered 40 miles – 60 road miles in just twenty-four hours.

By 18 September, the invasion of Poland was more or less sealed. The half-track had clearly demonstrated its effectiveness, not just as a weapon of war, but as a versatile machine that had kept up with the thrusting Panzers and supported the infantry as well.

Astonished by the successive gains of the Panzers and supporting armour, eight months later on 10 May 1940, Hitler finally decided to attack the west, which comprised the invasion of Holland, Belgium and Luxembourg.

For the attack against the west the German Army were divided into three army groups – Army Group A, B and C. The main strike would be given to Army Group A, which would drive its armoured units through the Ardennes, and then swing round across the plains of northern France and then make straight for the Channel coast, thereby cutting the Allied force in half and breaking the main enemy concentration in Belgium between Army Group A advancing from the south and Army Group B in the north. The task of Army Group B was to occupy Holland with motorized forces and to prevent the linking up of the Dutch army with the Anglo-Belgian force. It was to destroy the Belgian frontier defences by a rapid and powerful attack and throw the enemy back over the line between Antwerp and Namur. The fortress of Antwerp was to be surrounded from the north and east and the fortress of Liege from the north-east and north of the Meuse.

Army Group C, which was the most southern of the three army groups, was to engage the garrison of the Maginot Line, penetrating it if possible.

Apart from the masses of tanks and other armoured vehicles in the *Panzerwaffe*'s arsenal, to support the Blitzkrieg there was a single company of ten 88mm FlaK 18 on *Zugkraftwagen*. These 88mm flak guns were mounted on the chassis of an armoured Sd.Kfz.7 half-track in order to give much needed firepower support against the thickly armoured British Matilda and French Char B tanks.

By the end of the first day of the attack in the west, Belgian resistance had been overwhelmed and the cavalry of the French 9th Army brushed aside. Although the French 7th Army had reached Breda on 11 May by the next day it was in retreat under strong pressure from Guderian's Panzers. By evening of that same day, the Panzer units reached the Meuse along a 100-mile front, from Sedan to Dinant. They had advanced nearly 90 miles in three days. As the whole front began to crumble in indecision and confusion, the demoralized French Army tended to its wounds and withdrew to Antwerp along roads clogged with refugees. To the south, French troops immobilized at the Maginot Line were unable to move for the lack of transport, and were clearly unable to intervene against strong German forces.

By 15 May, the Dutch Army formally surrendered, although isolated units continued to fight a grim defensive battle until 17 May. As German troops occupied Holland with lightening speed, Belgium's capital finally capitulated.

The next day on 18 May, the 5th Panzer Division reported that it had reached the northern bank of the Sambre. Here armoured vehicles from Panzer-Regiment.31 began expanding their bridgehead north of the river. The 28.Infantry-Division pushed further west meeting spirited French resistance.

On other parts of the front the advance was progressing equally as well. General Heinz Guderian's reconnaissance had successfully crossed the River Somme and captured Peronne.

Within ten days the front lines in northern France were shrinking, cracking slowly but surely under the massive German pressure. German units seemed to be progressing with an increased determination and vigour, convinced of their ability to crush the enemy before it could prepare a secondary line of defence. In an unparalleled armoured dash, some units had covered more than 50 miles in just twenty-four hours.

By 14 June, the first German troops from the 9th Infantry-Division reported that they had arrived on the outskirts of Paris. Later that evening the division entered the French capital.

On 15 June, von Kleist's and Guderian's *Panzergruppe* reported that their armour was now advancing at breakneck speed on both sides of the Reims. These two powerful Panzer groups caused massive problems to retreating enemy formations. Guderian's tanks successfully reached Bar-sur-Aube and Gray-sur-Saone, while armour of the von Kleist group had driven its armoured might into Saint-Florentin and Tonnerre. Two days later, on 17 June, the right wing of Guderian's XXXIX Army Corps reached the Swiss border.

With the arrival of the German forces at the Swiss border, a ring was closed around the remaining French troops who were now frantically withdrawing from Lorraine and Alsace. Guderian was now able to move north-east and penetrate the Maginot fortifications from the rear using his powerful armoured units. In spite of determined French resistance along the Maginot Line, with its vast array of heavily constructed bunkers and well-armed fortifications, it was soon overrun and captured.

In the final days just before the French Army finally capitulated, the Germans continued their advance, smashing the enemy. By 20 June it was estimated that some 500,000 French soldiers had been captured. Large amounts of battlefield booty also fell into German hands.

To make the problems even greater for the French, the Italians had declared war on France, sending some thirty-two divisions against some six French divisions. However, against 185,000 troops, the Italians made little progress against well-trained French soldiers of the Alps.

A 1-ton Sd.Kfz.10 negotiates a hill whilst two crew members and their commanding officer enjoy the ride. Note the folded canvas and its framework, which was primarily used during bad weather.

During a training exercise probably in 1939 and the crew of an early variant Sd.Kfz.251 pose for the camera. The Sd.Kfz.251 was to become one of the most popular half-tracks used during the war not only to carry troops into battle, but to tow ordnance and stow other important equipment.

During a training exercise, more than likely just prior to the war, a Sd.Kfz.10 is being put through its paces. Onboard the half-track party officials and civilians are shown just how versatile the vehicle is across open terrain.

In this photograph the crew of a Sd.Kfz.8 show off the two-tone half-track as it negotiates a steep gradient during a training exercise. As with all vehicles during this early period of the war, the half-track has a camouflage scheme of dark grey.

A German parade, probably in Berlin on 20 April 1939, to mark Hitler's 50th birthday celebrations. The vehicles moving along the road passing the viewing stand comprise of the Sd.Kfz.7 and the new 150mm s.FH 18 howitzers.

In one of the many mobile workshops near the front, troops pose for the camera with their half-track. The engine compartment has been removed exposing the vehicles large engine. A hoist can be seen attached to the engine.

Two *Luftwaffe* crewmen pose for the camera in front of their Sd.Kfz.8 half-track during a pause in their advance through Holland. This vehicle is more than likely towing an 88mm FlaK gun to the battlefront.

Moving towards the front and an 8-ton Sd.Kfz.7 is hauling a 150mm s.FH 18 heavy field howitzer across a field. Note that the gun is configured for towing by motorized transport with rubber-rimmed wheels of the same size on both the carriage and limber.

A column of Sd.Kfz.7 half-tracks towing a s.FH 18 heavy field howitzers have halted on a road. This particular half-track was primarily designed to move the 88mm FlaK, as well as the 100mm s.K 18 and 150mm s.FH 18 into battle.

A half-track passes through one of the many destroyed towns and villages in western Poland during early September 1939. The troops onboard are all armed with the standard Mauser 98K bolt action rifle and will probably dismount from the half-track once they near enemy positions.

A Sd.Kfz.6 advances along a sandy Polish road during operations in September 1939. The vehicle is towing a pontoon bridging section which suggests this is an engineer bridging section unit.

Advancing through a captured town is a Sd.Kfz.251/1 following a Sd.Kfz.10 light half-track. Note the divisional insignia painted on the rear of the Sd.Kfz.251 indicating that it belongs to the 1.Panzer-Division.

A Sd.Kfz.7, probably operating either in Poland or France, advances along a road with a small compliment of crew. The canvas foul weather cover has been removed so that it allows easy access for the crew to quickly board and dismount and allow all round visibility under battlefield conditions.

A Sd.Kfz.8 has halted on a road and the gun crew of a Mortar 18 carriage for a 170mm or 210mm piece take a much needed rest on a grassy verge. Note that the gun carriage the half-track is towing is fitted with wheels and a limber that were normally seen on a horse-drawn piece.

During operations on the Western Front in 1940 and a Sd.Kfz.251 half-track belonging to the 1.Panzer-Division advances along a road passing a stationary StuG.III.Ausf.A, which was making its debut on the battlefield that summer.

A *Luftwaffe* crew of a Sd.Kfz.7 have parked their vehicle next to a building, probably during operations on the Western Front. The half-track is well camouflaged. Note the two registration plates attached to the front fender.

A well camouflaged *Luftwaffe* Sd.Kfz.7 half-track travels through a town towing what appears to be an 88mm FlaK gun. The 88mm FlaK gun was a very deadly and effective piece of weaponry and scored sizable hits both in an anti-aircraft and ground assault setting.

A *Wehrmacht* soldier poses for the camera on a road next to a stationary Sd.Kfz.7, which is hauling a s.FH 18 heavy field howitzer.

A Sd.Kfz.7 hauling a s.FH 18 howitzer crosses over a pontoon bridge towards the front lines. By May 1940, the Sd.Kfz.7 was used extensively during the conquest of Holland, Belgium and France. It was used primarily to pull heavy ordnance such as the s.FH 18, the 105mm and the 170mm or 210mm Mörsers.

A column of vehicles negotiate a dusty road. Leading the drive is a Sd.Kfz.7 towing a s.FH 18 heavy field howitzer. Its carriage and limber are clearly designed for animal draught.

Moving along a road towards the front lines is an 8-ton Sd.Kfz.7 medium half-track, towing a 150mm s.FH 18 heavy field howitzer. During the campaign in the West, the half-track transformed the fighting quality of the artillery batteries and enabled gun crews to support the advancing armoured spearheads with less difficulty than using animal draught.

A Sd.Kfz.7 has more than likely been utilized in a clear-up operation following heavy bomb damage to an urbanized area. Some of the crew can be seen observing the damage to a building, who are standing among civilians, some of which are children.

A Sd.Kfz.7 with a mounted four-barrelled light FlaK gun has halted inside a town. This weapon was very powerful and was capable of firing 1,800 rounds per minute, making it a deadly flak gun not just against low flying aircraft, but also ground targets as well.

Here *Wehrmacht* troops prepare to board a Sd.Kfz.251 Ausf.A variant, which can be identified by the three ports on each side of the upper armoured superstructure. Many of these early variants generally did not have the shielded MG34 machine gun attached to a sustained fire mount, as in this case.

The crew of a Sd.Kfz.7 can be seen halted on a hill, watching *Wehrmacht* troops salvage supplies, including ammunition from a truck that has toppled over and collided with another supply vehicle.

Probably part of a *Gebirgsjäger* pioneer unit assisting in pushing a supply vehicle with trailer along a temporary road surface. Nearby the crew of a Sd.Kfz.7 watch the spectacle from the comfort of their vehicle.

A Sd.Kfz.6/2 advances through a village somewhere in northern France in late May 1940. This *Luftwaffe* half-track is armed with an un-shielded 37mm FlaK 36. Less than 200 of these vehicles ever saw active service in the *Luftwaffe*, but nonetheless were very successful combating both aerial and ground targets.

A Sd.Kfz.7 with armoured body advances along a road hauling a modified 88mm FlaK 18 on a Sd.Ah.201 limber. These flak guns served well during the French campaign and scored considerable success owing to the rapid transportability of the weapon to the front lines.

A column of half-track vehicles comprising Sd.Kfz.7 are stationary beside a road. By 1940, the half-track had become a necessity on the battlefield. With the bulk of the *Wehrmacht* still relying heavily of animal draught, the Germans used the half-track extensively not only to tow ordnance and other supplies, but to carry troops to the forward edge of the battlefield.

This Sd.Kfz.7 can be seen hauling an 88mm FlaK 18 on its Sd.Ah.201 limber across uneven ground. Note the non-standard tarpaulin erected over the drivers compartment. This has obviously been done in order to keep the sun off the driver.

A Sd.Kfz.7 towing an 88mm FlaK 18 passes a gun crew during the campaign in France. The half-track probably belongs to a *Luftwaffe* unit. Note the kill rings painted in yellow on the flak gun's 88mm barrel.

A Sd.Kfz.7 hauls a 150mm s.FH 15cm heavy field howitzer towards the battlefront. Whilst half-tracks were more than capable of moving heavy weaponry from one part of the front quickly and effectively, much of the motive power in 1940 was still animal draught.

An interesting photograph showing a Sd.Kfz.7 towing a light Horch country vehicle along a dirt track. The half-track has its foul weather tarp pulled up in order to keep the crew and driver dry.

A Sd.Kfz.7 tows a s.FH 15cm heavy field howitzer along a dirt road. Foliage has been applied to the field howitzer's carriage and limber in order to break up its distinctive shape and limit the possibility of an air strike on the vehicle and its advancing column.

A Sd.Kfz.7 hauling a s.FH 15cm heavy field howitzer can be seen crossing a pontoon bridge during the French campaign. Reasonably good weather is predicted as the vehicles canvas foul weather cover has been removed.

An interesting photograph showing an early production model 8-ton Sd.Kfz.7 half-track. It hauls a 150mm s.FH 18 towards the battlefront.

What appears to be a *Luftwaffe* Sd.Kfz.7 towing an 88mm FlaK 18 gun stationary inside a French town, which, by the state of one of the buildings, has seen some considerable fighting. A column of horse drawn carts pass along the road trudging westward.

Chapter Two

1941

For the invasion of Russia, code-named Barbarossa, the German Army assembled some 3,000,000 men, divided into a total of 105 infantry divisions and 32 Panzer divisions. There were 3,332 tanks, over 7,000 artillery pieces, 50,000 motor vehicles, 625,000 horses, and some 10,000 half-track vehicles. This force was distributed into three German army groups: Army Group North, commanded by Field Marshal Wilhelm Ritter von Leeb, had assembled his forces in East Prussia on the Lithuanian frontier. His *Panzergruppe*, which provided the main spearhead for the advance on Leningrad, consisted of 812 tanks. These were divided among the 1, 6 and 8.Panzer-Divisions, 3, 36.Motorized-Infantry-Division and the SS.Motorized-Division '*Totenkopf*', which formed the *Panzergruppe* reserve.

For the Russian offensive, the Panzer divisions had been slightly modified in armoured firepower. They had been in fact diluted in strength in order to form the deployment of more divisions. The planners thought that, by concentrating a number of Panzer divisions together, they were able to achieve a massive local superiority. Spread among the Panzer divisions for support were the various half-tracks comprising of the Sd.Kfz.2, 7, 8, 9, 10, and 11. To provide armoured reconnaissance troops in the *Panzergrenadier* divisions with flexible armoured off road flexibility, hundreds of Sd.Kfz.250 supported the drive east. The Sd.Kfz.251 too was also used extensively in the attack against the Soviet Union.

The Panzer divisions contained one tank regiment of two, sometimes three *abteilungen*, totaling some 150–200 tanks; two motorized rifle (*schützen*) regiments, each of two battalions, whose infantry were carried in armoured half-tracks or similar vehicles, and a reconnaissance battalion of three companies (one motorcycle, two armoured car). The motorized infantry divisions accompanying the Panzer divisions in the *Panzergruppe* were similarly organized, but severely lacked armoured support. The divisional artillery comprised of two field, one medium and one anti-tank regiment and an anti-aircraft battalion. These were all motorized and more than capable of keeping up with the fast moving pace of the Panzers. All of the components that made up a fully-fledged Panzer division comprised of various half-tracks and artillery prime movers.

During the early morning of 22 June 1941, the German Army unleashed the maelstrom that was Barbarossa. After a month of victorious progress, the German armies were fighting on a front 1,000 miles wide. Along the entire front the half-tracks had exploited the terrain and had progressed at considerable speed. Yet in spite of these successes, the half-tracks were very thinly spread, and the bulk of the transportation still had to be undertaken by animal draught.

Nevertheless, between June and late September 1941, the Panzer and motorized divisions were more or less unhindered by lack of supply, difficult terrain or bad weather conditions. However, on 6 October, the first snowfall of the approaching winter was reported. It melted quickly, but turned the dirt roads into quagmires and rivers into raging torrents. The Russian autumn with its heavy rain, sleet and snow had arrived. The armoured drive east began to slow. Wheeled vehicles soon became stuck in a sea of mud and could only advance with the aid of tracked vehicles towing them. No preparations had been made for the winter and the Panzer divisions lacked the most basic supplies for cold weather. There were no chains available for towing vehicles, and no anti-freeze for the engine's coolant systems. Tank and infantrymen alike had no winter clothing either.

In blizzard conditions, where temperatures fell to 30 degrees below zero, the exhausted Panzer divisions soon ran out of fuel and ammunition, and were compelled to break off their attack within sight of Moscow. On 6 December, all plans to capture the Russian capital in 1941 had to be abandoned.

By the end of 1941, the battle weary divisions of the *Panzerwaffe*, which had taken part in Operation Barbarossa, were no longer fit to fight. Mobile operations had consequently ground to a halt. Fortunately for the exhausted Panzer crews and supporting half-track units, no mobile operations had been planned during the winter of 1941, let alone for 1942. In the freezing arctic temperatures, the majority of the Panzer divisions were pulled out of their stagnant defensive positions and transferred to France to rest, reorganize and retrain.

As for the half-tracks, these continued to be used extensively throughout the winter of 1941. The *Wehrmacht* and *Waffen-SS* owed much to their versatility on the battlefield. Many of the vehicles were used to transport troops from one sector of the front to another. Others assisted in towing heavy artillery or vitals supplies, where animal draught had failed due to terrain or the extreme arctic conditions.

An interesting photograph showing a Sd.Kfz.251/1 Ausf.B preparing to cross a river during operations on the Eastern Front during the summer of 1941. Note the number of Pioneers assisting the vehicles through the water.

A Sd.Kfz.251/1 Ausf.A is being put through its paces during summer fighting somewhere on the Eastern Front in 1941. This vehicle features the standard gun shield on the forward mount, but no MG34 machine gun is apparently fitted.

Moving steadily across rough terrain is a Sd.Kfz.251/6 Ausf.B. The vehicle is fitted with a special frame antenna. Note the spare track links attached to the front of the half-track for additional armoured protection.

A column of vehicles negotiates a very muddy road following a heavy downpour of rain. A Pz.Kpfw.I tank has halted in the mire and one the crew members watches a support vehicle and a pair of Sd.Kfz.7 half-tracks move along the road.

A pair of Sd.Kfz.7 half-tracks, both with a foul weather tarpaulin, advance along a muddy road. Even during the summer periods on the Eastern Front a heavy downpour could easily delay or halt an entire armoured column.

A Sd.Kfz.10/4 armed with a 20mm FlaK 30 has pulled-up inside a wooded area in order to conceal itself from both ground and aerial observation. The 20mm FlaK 30 can be easily identified by the asymmetrical splinter shields, which confirms this vehicle as a 10/4 variant.

An armoured column approaches what appears to be a concrete obstacle topped with barbed wire. An early production model StuG.III leads the column. Behind the StuG.III is what appears to be a Sd.Kfz.251.Ausf.A.

A column of various vehicles from the 2.Panzer-Division on a road somewhere on the Eastern Front. Alongside a Pz.Kpfw.III Ausf.J, two Sd.Kfz.10s can be seen with a full complement of crew.

Bitter fighting in the East during the relentless summer battles of 1941 and a Sd.Kfz.253 can be seen halted on a road. Its crew observe the battle unfolding in the distance through a pair of 6 × 30 field binoculars. This vehicle was a battery command and observation vehicle attached to one of the new *Sturmgeschütz* units.

A Sd.Kfz.252 passes through a destroyed town somewhere in the East. The Sd.Kfz.250 was designed to provide armoured reconnaissance troops to the *Panzer* and *Panzergrenadier* divisions with a flexible armoured vehicle that possessed better off road capability than the Sd.Kfz.222 armoured cars.

A *Mittlerer Zugkraftwagen* 8-ton Sd.Kfz.7 prime mover hauls an 88mm FlaK gun towards the battlefront during the summer battles in the East in 1941. These half-tracks were widely used in Russia not only to tow FlaK guns, but 100mm s.K 18 and 150mm s.FH 18 artillery as well. They were regarded by both the *Wehrmacht* and *Waffen-SS* as the workhorse half-track of the Second World War.

Along the front line during a heavy enemy contact, a number of Sd.Kfz.251 half-track personnel carriers can be seen with a Pz.Kpfw.III. Smoke can be seen rising into the air following a shell impact. It is difficult to tell whether the explosion has been caused by enemy aerial or ground contact.

Wehrmacht troops who have aided an injured comrade take cover behind a Sd.Kfz.252. There were twelve different variants of the Sd.Kfz.250 series of half-tracks, two of which were issued to the *Sturmgeschütz* units. One of them carried ammunition, known officially as the Sd.Kfz.252, and the other was a battery command and observation vehicle, known as the Sd.Kfz.253.

A photograph taken during a training exercise. A number of Sd.Kfz.251 half-track personnel carriers, two of which can be seen mounted with the MG34 machine gun and splinter shield, approach two infantry dugout positions. One position is defended by a light MG34 and the other with a Karabiner 98K bolt action rifle.

A Sd.Kfz.252 advances through a Yugoslavian town passing what appears to be local women in their native wear, lining the street and greeting the German column into their town. Some flowers have been adorned to the half-track by the local populace, probably more for German propaganda than the Yugoslavians.

A Platoon commander can be seen shouting out a signal to his troops as his Sd.Kfz.250/10 Ausf.A variant moves toward the battlefront. These half-tracks were fitted with the 37mm PaK 36, together with gun shield and sight.

A group of officers confer with the aid of maps sitting at the side of a road. Behind them are a motorcycle, motorcycle combination and a stationary Sd.Kfz.251 armed with mounted MG34 machine gun and splinter shield.

Advancing through a captured town is an Sd.Kfz.251 accompanied by two motorcycles. Painted in white or yellow on the rear of the vehicle is the letter 'G', which indicates that this half-track is attached to General Guderian's *Panzergruppe 2*. This photograph was more than likely taken during summer operations on the Eastern Front in 1941.

This Sd.Kfz.7 is pulling an 88mm FlaK 18 on a Sd.Ah 201 limber. The vehicle has rod style grab handles mounted between the row of seats in order to allow quick mounting and dismounting by the crew.

Two Sd.Kfz.251 armoured personnel carriers with *Panzergrenadiers* advance towards the frontline. This was one of the quickest and most effective means for troops to enter the forward edge of the battlefield onboard a half-track.

Two Sd.Kfz.7 prime movers haul 150mm s.FH howitzers through the snow during winter operations in Russia in November or December 1941. The two trucks in between the half-tracks probably carry ammunition for the howitzers.

In the depths of the Russian winter in December 1941 is a Sd.Kfz.7 towing an 88mm FlaK gun along a snowy road. The vehicle still retains its original dark grey camouflage scheme. Note the letter 'G' on the windshield indicating that it belongs to 'Guderian's *Panzergruppe* 2'.

The crew of a Sd.Kfz.10 rest with their vehicle. The half-track has been purposely parked in dense overgrowth in order to help conceal it from either ground or aerial detection. All the troops are wearing the standard M1938 field cap.

A Sd.Kfz.7 has halted inside a newly captured town somewhere on the Eastern Front. By the appearance of littered wreckage along the road there has been some significant fighting in the area.

Three crewmen pose for the camera in front of their prime mover during winter operations on the Eastern Front in December 1941. This artillery tractor has been finished in overall dark grey with no visible markings.

The crew of an artillery tractor pose for the camera in front of their vehicle during winter operations on the Eastern Front. The crew has applied whitewash camouflage paint over the entire vehicle in order to try and conceal it in the snow.

An 8-ton Sd.Kfz.7 is hauling a 105mm l.FH 18 field howitzer across a pontoon bridge. The 105mm field howitzer provided the division with a relatively effective mobile base of fire. It was primarily the artillery regiments that were given the task of destroying enemy positions and fortified defences and conducting counter-battery fire prior to an armoured assault.

A Sd.Kfz.253 negotiates a small wooden bridge. This vehicle's intended role was as a command and observation vehicle for a *Sturmgeschütz* battery. The radio antenna can be seen attached to the vehicle, which enabled the crew to communicate with other vehicles in the field including the command post.

Out in a field and the crew of a Sd.Kfz.10/4 observe enemy aerial activity. The gun's commander uses a pair of binoculars to track the target, whilst another crewmember uses a range finder. Mounted onboard the half-track is an un-shielded 20mm FlaK 30 elevated and prepared for firing.

At the side of a road stand the destroyed remains of a Sd.Kfz.251/1 Ausf.A. The vehicle has obviously received a direct hit in the rear compartment area. The tracks have been ripped off in the explosion along with one of the front tyres.

A Sd.Kfz.7/1 armed with the quadruple 20mm gun FlaK 38 leads a column of vehicles along a road during summer operations in Russia. The crew have applied foliage to parts of the vehicle in order to break up its distinctive shape and reduce the possibility of it being attacked by aircraft.

A Sd.Kfz.250/1 Ausf.A advances through a city. The vehicle has been fitted with an MG34 machine gun complete with fifty-round basket drum magazine. The Sd.Kfz.250 was a light armoured personnel carrier for reconnaissance duties.

In the depths of the Russian winter and a Sd.Kfz.251 armoured personnel carrier with a full complement of *Panzergrenadiers* onboard follow a *Horch* cross country car and a Pz.Kpfw.III.

Two *Luftwaffe* crewmen, one equipped with skis, pose for the camera in front of a Sd.Kfz.7 half-track. This 8-ton tractor still bears the old dark grey camouflage scheme and no attempt has been made to use winter whitewash paint.

A Sd.Kfz.7 has halted in the snow. The prime mover is towing a 37mm FlaK gun. This weapon was used in conjunction with light flak, often to protect important military installations. It was widely used by *Luftwaffe* flak units.

A Sd.Kfz.7 can be seen in the snow. The vehicle still retains its old dark grey camouflage paint and there are no other markings.

On a pontoon bridge and the crew of a Sd.Kfz.7 half-track pose for the camera. During the war much was owed to the half-track, which remained until the end of the war a very versatile, sturdy and reliable machine, often salvaging men and equipment from near destruction.

A Sd.Kfz.7 advances across a tract of sandy soil creating a dust cloud that could be easily identified by aerial observation. On the Eastern Front in particular, especially during the summer periods when the land was very dry, large columns of armoured vehicles often produced immense dust clouds, which regularly gave away the advance to the enemy.

Chapter Three

1942

In spite of the terrible problems that faced the badly depleted Panzer divisions, back in Germany production of tanks and half-track vehicles still increased. In order to overcome the mammoth task of defeating the Red Army, more Panzer divisions were being raised, and motorized divisions converted into *Panzergrenadier* divisions. Although equipping the *Panzerwaffe* was a slow and expensive process, it was undertaken effectively with the introduction of a number of new, fresh divisions being deployed on the front lines.

However, by the beginning of the summer offensive in May 1942, not all the Panzer divisions were fully equipped and ready for combat. Some of the older units, for instance, did not even have their losses from the winter offensive of 1941 replaced and were not ready for any type of full-scale operation. Worn out and depleted Panzer divisions were therefore relegated to Army Group North or Army Group Centre, where they were hastily deployed for a series of defensive actions instead. The best-equipped Panzer divisions were shifted south to Army Group South for operations through Caucasus. It was entrusted to the two Panzer Armies – 1st and 4th – that were to spearhead the drive. By May 1942, most of the Panzer divisions involved were up to nearly eighty-five per cent of their original fighting strength.

With renewed confidence, the summer offensive, codenamed 'Operation Blau', opened up in southern Russia. Some fifteen Panzer divisions and *Panzergrenadier* divisions of the 1st and 4th Armies, together with Italian, Rumanian and Hungarian formations crashed into action. In just two days the leading spearheads had pushed 150km deep into the enemy lines and had begun to cut off the city of Voronezh. The city fell on 7 July. The two Panzer armies then converged with all its might on Stalingrad. It seemed that the Russians were now doomed. With an air of confidence, Hitler decided to abandon the armoured advance on Stalingrad and embark on an encirclement operation down on the Don. The 6th Army was to go on and capture Stalingrad without any real Panzer support and fight a bloody battle of attrition there. Eventually the fighting became so fierce it embroiled some twenty-one German divisions including six Panzer and *Panzergrenadier* divisions.

The 6th Army soon became encircled and three hurriedly reorganized under strength Panzer divisions were thrown into a relief operation. By 19 December the 6th Panzer Division had fought its way to within 50km of Stalingrad. But under increasing Russian pressure the relief operation failed. The 6th Panzer Division and remnants of the 4th Panzer Army were forced to retreat, leaving the 6th Army in the encircled city to its fate. Some 94,000 soldiers surrendered on 2 February 1943. With them the 14th, 16th, and 24th Panzer Divisions, and the 3rd, 29th, and 60th *Panzergrenadier* Divisions were decimated.

A Sd.Kfz.10/4 with a mounted 20mm FlaK gun has halted on a road somewhere on the Eastern Front in 1942. The side gun platform has been folded down to provide additional space for the crew to manoeuvre around the gun.

A new Sd.kfz.251 Ausf.A, more than likely on a training exercise, manoeuvres along a sandy tract of land. This photograph gives a very good view of the MG34 machine gun on its sustained fire mount.

A SdKfz.7 half-track has just driven off a pontoon bridge during its armoured column's drive eastward. Next to the half-track is a Pz.Kpfw.II. Throughout the war, the SdKfz.7 proved a useful supplement to the predominantly truck-borne rifle infantry of the Panzer divisions. It was able to maintain speed across country and keep up with the fast-moving Panzer units.

More than likely troops of the 4th *SS-Polizei-Division* during operations in Army Group North in 1942. A stationary Sd.Kfz.8 half-track can be seen parked next to a Pz.Kpfw.III of the 4.Company of a Panzer Regiment.

A Sd.Kfz.10/4 armed with a mounted 20mm FlaK gun moves along a sandy embankment somewhere in Russia. On the folding sides of the half-track additional magazines for the gun are carried and a single axle trailer stowing more vital equipment and magazines were usually stored. This particular half-track probably provided support to one of the Panzer divisions during their advance through Russia.

An interesting photograph showing the Sd.Kfz.251 modified Ausf.C variant operating on the Eastern Front. This particular variant is armed with the 20mm FlaK 38 gun complete with splinter shield. The insignia indicates that it belongs to the famous *Grossdeutchland* Division. Parked next to the half-track, the commander of a StuG.III scans the sky for enemy aircraft.

A Sd.Kfz.251 armoured personnel carrier wades through a stream following in close support of an Sd.kfz.10 towing a PaK gun. Festooned to the Sd.Kfz.251's front are logs. This was to prevent the sinking of the half-track's front wheels in soft or marshy ground.

A battery of Sd.Kfz.10/4 armed with mounted 20mm FlaK guns are in action against an enemy target. The hinged sides have been completely removed for combat in order to allow the crew plenty of space to use the gun and reload with ammunition. Anti-aircraft defences came into prominence by September 1941, as the Soviet Air Force started to inflict heavier casualties.

A photograph taken from inside a moving Sd.Kfz.251. A *Panzergrenadier* can be seen with his MG34 mounted on a sustained fire mount. The vehicle is racing across a large field following a column of Pz.Kpfw.IIs.

A pair of crewman preparing their *Panzerwerfer* for a fire mission in the snow. This vehicle was known by the Germans as the *Maultier* ('Mule'). This particular 'Mule' is armed with a ten-tube 150mm *Nebelwerfer* 42. Some 300 of these half-track *Panzerwerfer*'s entered service, mainly for the Eastern Front.

A Sd.Kfz.251 armoured personnel carrier has halted on a road next to a destroyed building. A *Panzergrenadier* can be seen armed with a M1924 stick grenade standing next to the building and poised to throw the grenade through the window.

A Sd.Kfz.10/4 half-track has halted outside a village. The sides of the gun platform have been lowered suggesting that this vehicle is about to be embroiled in action against an enemy target. Note the letter 'K' painted on the rear of ammunition trailer, partially obscured by the troop's leg, indicating that this vehicle is attached to *'Panzergruppe Kleist'*.

An interesting photograph showing a half-track *Panzerwerfer* being prepared for action on the Eastern Front. This *Nebelwerfer* launch vehicle has an application of whitewash camouflage paint, and the letter 'G' on the sides and rear of the superstructure probably indicates that it's the seventh launcher in a battery of eight.

A retouched image showing *Wehrmacht* troops in a dug out position waiting to go into action. In the foreground is a Sd.Kfz.251 armoured personnel carrier. It was primarily the success of the Sd.Kfz.251 in the early war years that afforded half-tracks a frontline combat role alongside the Panzer on the Eastern Front.

A number of half-tracks can be seen near a main rail head somewhere in Russia during summer operations. Throughout the war on the Eastern Front, the half-track offered troops armoured protection and mobility. The use of the half-track was an example of rapid tactical deployment that changed the way battles were fought forever.

From his Sd.Kfz.251 a commanding officer orders his men into action. The Sd.Kfz.251 became the most popular vehicle used by the *Panzergrenadiers* and was frequently seen in the thick of battle, moving alongside tanks and providing them with valuable support.

Dressed in their winter reversibles, these troops are preparing a position in the frozen ground next to a Sd.Kfz.6/2 half-track armed with a 37mm FlaK gun. It was not until Russia, when soldiers were given greater combat roles, that the half-tracks were equipped with heavier main armaments to give them even greater offensive punch.

A Sd.Kfz.7/1 mounting a quadruple-barrelled FlaK gun is concealed in a field. This weapon demonstrated outstanding anti-aircraft capabilities. Though these weapons were used in both ground and aerial roles, in an anti-tank function they were not particularly effective against heavy Russian armour.

Dispersed in the open and a Sd.Kfz.10 half-track armed with the 20mm FlaK 30 can be seen in action against an enemy target. The crew are well placed behind the gun. Note the discarded gas mask canisters placed in a line on the ground. It is probable that, due to the restricted space onboard the vehicle, the crew have temporarily discarded them.

A SS flak gunner scours the skies for Soviet aircraft. He is standing on the decking of a Sd.Kfz.7/1, which mounts a 20mm quadruple-barrelled anti-aircraft gun. Note the kill markings displayed on the gun shield.

An interesting photograph showing a number of Sd.Kfz.10/4 half-tracks towing 50mm PaK 38 guns towards the front. In the foreground are two stationary Sd.Kfz.7 with 150mm howitzers on tow that have halted in a field.

Vehicles belonging to Kleist's *'Panzergruppe'* are seen operating in a deserted Russian town, recently captured by this column. Two Pz.Kpfw.IIs can be seen with a Pz.Kpfw.III and two Sd.Kfz.251 armoured personnel carriers.

A well concealed Sd.Kfz.6/2 being prepared for a fire mission. This vehicle was initially designed as an engineer equipment and personnel carrier. However, because of the prolonged war on the Eastern Front, they were quickly adapted to haul various ordnance and to mount a 37mm FlaK gun, as in this photograph.

An Sd.Kfz.10/4 has halted on a road, somewhere in southern Russia. The vehicle is armed with a 20mm FlaK gun and the sides are folded up, indicating no signs of enemy aerial or ground activity.

Advancing across a vast open space in southern Russia are a number of armoured vehicles including a Pz.Kpfw.I and two Sd.Kfz.7s hauling 88mm FlaK guns. By 1942/43, the extensive use of 88mm FlaK guns were in prominence as heavier enemy armour was encountered by the Germans on a daily basis. Growing enemy aerial activity too became unceasing.

An Sd.Kfz.251 armoured personnel carrier is seen on a road somewhere in Russia. The letter 'G' on one of its blacked out headlamps indicates that it belongs to 'Guderian's *Panzergruppe*'. Note the sand bags on the vehicle in order to help protect the crew from enemy fire.

A Sd.Kfz.250/3 complete with long range radio antenna can be seen hurtling along a road at speed. The vehicle is partly camouflaged with foliage in order to try and break up the half-track's distinctive shape.

Various vehicles can be seen fording a river during operations on the Eastern Front. One of vehicles is a Sd.Kfz.251 armoured personnel carrier. The half-track, especially the Sd.Kfz.251, was a very versatile vehicle and could often travel across some of the most rugged terrain.

Half-track, Sd.Kfz.251/3, during operations on the Eastern Front in 1942. There were a number of versions of this particular vehicle, two of which were used by *Luftwaffe* personnel for air coordination. It is probable that this half-track is in cooperation with nearby aircraft. Note the tow cable and spare road wheel attached to the side of the vehicle for additional armoured protection. This half-track is covered in a base coat of dark yellow with a heavy over-sprayed mottle pattern of olive green, red and brown.

Four more photographs showing the crew of the same half-track, Sd.Kfz.251/3, during operations on the Eastern Front in 1942.

Somewhere in Russia and a column of armoured vehicles, comprising a Sd.Kfz.252, are following a pair of StuG.IIIs. The half-track is towing an Sd.Ah. 3-1/1 trailer which has a tactical marking painted in yellow, indicating it's assigned to a *Sturmgeschütz* battery.

Advancing along a road with its foul weather tarp up is a Sd.Kfz.8 towing a *Mörserlafette* 18 carriage for a 170mm or 210mm piece. This 12-ton vehicle was primarily designed to tow heavier artillery such as the 170mm s.K 18, 210mm Morser 18 and 105mm FlaK 39.

Chapter Four

1943

Throughout the early cold months of 1943, the *Panzerwaffe* built up strength of the badly depleted Panzer divisions. By the summer they fielded some twenty-four Panzer divisions on the Eastern Front alone. This was a staggering transformation of a Panzer force that had lost immeasurable amounts of armour in less than two years of combat. Hitler now intended to risk his precious *Panzerwaffe* in what became the largest tank battle of the Second World War, Operation *Zitadelle*.

For the offensive Hitler was determined to put together a massive array of armour. However, the *Panzerwaffe* of 1943 were unlike those armoured forces that had victoriously steamrolled across western Russia two years earlier. The losses during the previous winter had resulted in the drastic reductions in troop strength. Despite the *Panzerwaffe*'s impressive array of firepower, this shortage of infantry was to lead to Panzer units being required to take on more ambitious tasks normally preserved for the infantry. In fact, to make matters worse, by the time the final date had been set for the attack as the 4 July, the Red Army knew the German plans and had already made their preparations. For three long months there had been extensive building and various other preparations to counter the German attack. Improved intelligence allowed Russian commanders to predict exactly the strategic focal point of the German attack. The *Panzerwaffe*, however, were determined to rejuvenate their *Blitzkrieg* tactics, but the immense preparations that had gone into constructing the Soviet defences meant that the *Panzerwaffe* were never going to succeed in penetrating into the strategic depths of the Red Army fortifications with any overriding success.

When the attack was finally unleashed in the pre-dawn light of 5 July 1943, the Germans were stunned by the dogged defence of their Red foe. The battle was unlike any other engagement they had previously encountered and within a matter of days, the Red Army had ground down the mighty *Panzerwaffe* and threw its offensive timetable off schedule. Through sheer weight of Soviet strength and stubborn combat along an ever-extending front, the German mobile units were finally forced to a standstill.

The losses that the *Panzerwaffe* sustained at Kursk were so immense that it undoubtedly led to the German Army taking their first steps of its slow retreat back towards Germany. The Russians had managed to destroy no less than thirty divisions, seven of which were Panzer. German reinforcements were insufficient to replace the staggering losses, so they fought on under-strength.

The reverberations caused by the defeat at Kursk meant that German forces in the south bore the brunt of the heaviest Soviet drive. Both the Russian city of Voronezh and Steppe Fronts possessed massive local superiority against everything the Germans had on the battlefield, and this included their diminishing resources of tanks and assault guns. The *Panzerwaffe* were now duty-bound to improvise with what they had at their disposal and try to maintain themselves in the field, and in doing so they hoped to wear the enemy's offensive capacity. But in the south where the weight of the Soviet effort was directed, Army Group South's line began breaking and threatened to be ripped wide open. Stiff defensive action was now the stratagem placed upon the *Panzerwaffe*, but they lacked sufficient reinforcements and the strength of their armoured units dwindled steadily as they tried to hold back the Russian might.

In only a matter of three months since the defeat at Kursk, Army Centre and South had been pushed back an average distance of 150 miles on a 650-mile front. Despite heavy resistance in many sectors of the front, the Soviets lost no time in exploiting the fruits of regaining as much territory as possible. In Army Group South, where the frontlines threatened to completely cave in under intense enemy pressure, frantic appeals to Hitler were made by Field Marshal Manstein to withdraw his forces across the Dnieper River. What followed was a fighting withdrawal that degenerated into a race with the Russians for possession of the river. Whilst the Panzer divisions covered the rear, the army group's columns withdrew on selected river crossing points at Cherkassy, Dnepropetrovsk, Kiev, Kanev and Kremenchug, leaving behind a burnt and blasted wasteland during their retreat.

The winter of 1943 opened with a frustrating series of deliberations for the *Panzerwaffe*. Much of its concerns were centred around preventing the awesome might of the Red Army with what little they had available at their disposal. Yet, in October and November of 1943, only five Panzer divisions and one SS Panzer division were sent as replacements to the Eastern Front.

During the winter of 1943, all units on the Eastern Front averaged some 2,000 tanks and 700 half-tracks. It was indeed a very small force for such a large front to cover but, despite the depressing statistics, the German tank soldiers were still infused with confidence and the ability to hold ground.

By early November the Russians once again pushed forward across the wet and snowy plains in the south. In the wake of a massive artillery bombardment, Soviet forces hit the centre of the German front with such force that it ripped it open. What followed was a bitter and bloody battle by the Germans to try and stabilize the front.

Throughout December the *Panzerwaffe* fought well, and at times even succeeded in surprising Red Army forces with a number of daring attacks of their own. But in spite of these successes, the *Panzerwaffe* were hard pressed to contain their growing enemy.

Here a Sd.Kfz.10/4 mounting a 20mm FlaK gun advances at speed along a road. Note all the sides are up with intact ammunition magazines attached to the sides for easy access. The photograph illustrates just how cramped conditions could be for the crew whilst travelling.

A column of Sd.Kfz.251 armoured personnel carriers are seen advancing through a village somewhere on the Eastern Front. In the foreground are what appear to be two Pz.Kpfw.IV Ausf.H variants. One of them still retains its summer camouflage scheme, whilst the other has its winter whitewash paint.

A Sd.Kfz.251 speeds along a road passing burning Russian artillery. The Sd.Kfz.251 was a very versatile half-track that was popular in both the *Wehrmacht* and *Waffen-SS* until the end of the war.

A 20mm FlaK gun crew moving to another position with their Sd.Kfz.10/4. The vehicle's sides are down and foliage has been applied to parts of the half-track and the Sd.Ah.51 ammunition trailer.

A Sd.kfz.11 can be seen hauling a 105mm l.FH 18 past a halted wheeled vehicle. Throughout the war the 105mm was used extensively by both the *Wehrmacht* and *Waffen-SS*. It was not only robust and versatile, but a very reliable gun.

A Sd.Kfz.251/1 Ausf.C advances past a destroyed building, which is burning. The half-track has its forward MG34 machine gun fixed to a sustained fire mount. Note that some of the crew have stored some of their personal equipment items on the superstructure sides. Space on these vehicles was always at a premium and crews were always utilizing what space they could find.

During operations in Army Group North on the Eastern Front is a Sd.Kfz.7 towing a trailer along a road filled with water. These troops more than likely belong to the 4th *SS-Polizei-Division*, which saw extensive action in the forests and swamps of northern Russia.

A photograph taken from onboard a Panther medium tank showing its commander looking down upon the crew of a Sd.Kfz.251/1 Ausd.D. The vehicle has camouflage netting attached for foliage to be easily attached and mounts an MG42 machine gun complete with gun shield.

Waffen-SS grenadiers in what appears to be a Sd.Kfz.251/7 Ausf.D. Note the MG42 machine gun mounted at the rear of the vehicle for local defence. This half-track was equipped with tools, explosives and assault bridge sections.

Advancing towards the battlefront is the *Funkpanzerwagen* Sd.Kfz.251/3 Ausf.C. This vehicle, complete with long range radio antenna, is armed with an MG34 machine gun. Some foliage has been applied to the antenna.

Two officers scan the terrain through a pair of 6 × 30 field binoculars. They stand on the engine deck of their Sd.Kfz.251/3 Ausf.C. The half-track is a command vehicle and is fitted with the standard long range antenna.

Three Sd.Kfz.251 half-tracks have halted somewhere on the vast Russian steppe somewhere in southern Russia. A soldier can be seen aided by two of his comrades after evidently being injured in battle.

This photograph clearly illustrates the versatility of a Sd.Kfz.6 as it moves across uneven ground. The six-cylinder Maybach HL54 TUKRM engine only produced 116hp, but gave it a top speed of 31mph on flat road surfaces. That speed was reduced significantly across rough terrain like this.

Two Sd.Kfz.251 armoured personnel carriers can be seen advancing through overgrowth during intensive fighting somewhere on the Eastern Front. Both these vehicles are covered in a base coat of dark yellow with a heavily over-sprayed mottle pattern of olive green, red and brown.

A Sd.Kfz.251 half-track follows a late variant Pz.Kpfw.IV towards the battlefront during summer operations on the Eastern Front. Extensive foliage covers the half-track in order to try and conceal it against both ground and aerial observation.

A Sd.Kfz.251/3 has halted next to a Sd.Kfz.250/3 in a field. The crew are conferring with what appear to be captured Russian troops. Both the vehicles have a summer camouflage scheme of a coat of dark yellow with a heavily over-sprayed mottle pattern of olive green, red and brown.

A photograph taken from a StuG.III Ausf.G with its powerful 75mm gun barrel. Spread out across the field as far as the eye can see are various armoured vehicles including the Sd.Kfz.251, Pz.Kpfw.III and Pz.Kpfw.IV.

Two Sd.Kfz.251/10 Ausf.A with a full shield on its 37mm PaK 36 are seen crossing a field during a heavy contact with the enemy. In the foreground, smoke can be seen rising into the air indicating heavy shelling to the area.

A crew member cleaning the 75mm KwK 37 L/24 gun barrel of his Sd.Kfz.251/9 Ausf.C prior to an enemy attack on the Eastern Front. This vehicle still retains some of its winter camouflage paint of white hand-painted dots.

An interesting photograph showing a column of Sd.Kfz.251/9 Ausf.C on a road destined for the front line. When the Pz.Kpfw.IV was up-armed with the 75mm KwK 40 L/43, the short 75mm KwK 37 L/24 gun barrel became redundant. However, it was soon decided that these short barrelled guns should be converted and mounted on a number of half-tracks, notably the 9 series of the Sd.Kfz.251.

Out in a field and the crew of a Sd.Kfz.7/1 prepares their *Flakvierling* 38 for action. On tow is a Sd.Ah.56 ammunition trailer. This half-track and trailer is covered in a base coat of dark yellow with a heavily over-sprayed mottle pattern of olive green.

Two Sd.Kfz.7/1 on the move somewhere in Russia. Both vehicles mount the lethal *Flakvierling* 38 with shield. The leading vehicle hauls the Sd.Ah.56 ammunition trailer. On the Eastern Front, the half-track undoubtedly transformed the fighting quality of artillery and flak batteries, enabling gun crews to support the advancing armoured spearheads with less difficulty.

Two motorcyclists and a light Horch cross-country car have halted on a dusty road. A Sd.Kfz.7 with a full crew passes by towing an 88mm FlaK 18 on a Sd.Ah 201 limber. Note one of the crewmen giving a traffic signal to approaching vehicles.

Here a Sd.Kfz.252 has been designated to accompany a *Sturmgeschütz* battery on the Eastern Front. In this photograph the half-track has pulled alongside a late variant StuG.III Ausf.G with its long barrelled 75mm StuK 40. One of the crew can be seen drinking from his canteen during a routine stop.

A Sd.Kfz.251 accompanies *Panzergrenadiers* into action. These armoured personnel carries were the most effective method of transportation for troops to reach the front lines without having to march many miles on foot, and then to set up positions and fight.

Panzergrenadiers are seen dismounting from a Sd.Kfz.251/1 Ausf.C and going into action. The Ausf.C is indentified by the shape of the cowls on the side of the engine compartment. Note the summer camouflage scheme of dark yellow with a heavily over-sprayed mottle pattern of olive green.

The crew of a Sd.Kfz.251 during a routine stop can be seen next to a building and some trees. Some of the crew's undergarments are seen hanging out to dry on a line erected between two trees. Note the M35 steel helmets attached to the side of the vehicle.

A Sd.Kfz.251 half-track rolls down a road. Behind the armoured personnel carrier is a motorcycle. Both riders wear the waterproof motorcycle coat which was double-breasted in design and was generously cut and intended to be worn over equipment. The motorcyclists were also issued with various types of goggles, which can be seen here being worn.

A number of armoured personnel carriers can be seen driving through a field. The Sd.Kfz.251/3 with radio antenna appears fully loaded with supplies. Note the divisional insignia of the 24th Panzer Division painted on the rear of the vehicle.

A Sd.Kfz.7 hauling a 105mm le.FH16 light field howitzer. This gun was the standard light artillery piece deployed in the artillery divisions on the Eastern Front. The wheels on the artillery piece consisted of a heavy duty cast steel with a solid rubber rim. This type of design allowed the gun to be towed at relatively high-speed by a motorized vehicle.

A long line of Sd.Kfz.251/7 Ausf.D mounted on special railway flatcars for shipment to the Eastern Front. By this period of the war travel by rail was very dangerous and normally undertaken during darkness in order to minimize the threat of aerial attack.

A whitewashed Sd.Kfz.7 hauling an un-camouflaged 88mm FlaK 36/37 on a Sd.Ah.203 limber. Note the kill markings on the gun's splinter shield, which are arranged under different silhouettes: an aircraft with twelve bars; AFV with fifteen; soft skin with seven; and a solitary credit for destroying an observation balloon.

Chapter Five

1944

Throughout January and February, the winter did nothing to impede the Soviet offensives from grinding further west. At the beginning of March 1944, Army Group A and South still held about half the ground between the Dnieper and Bug rivers but, in a number of areas, the front was buckling under the constant strain of repeated Soviet attacks. As a consequence, Army Group South was being slowly pressed westwards, its Panzers still unable to strike a decisive counter-blow because of the Führer's order to stand fast on unsuitable positions. By 24 March, the Russians had spearheaded to the Dniester, and a few days later were penetrating the foothills of the Carpathians. *Panzerwaffe* units, that were refused by Hitler to withdraw, found themselves tied down trying in vain to hold back the Soviet avalanche. These battles became known to the Panzer soldiers as the 'cauldron battles' or *Kesselschlachten*.

By April mud finally brought an end to the almost continuous fighting in the south, and there was respite for the *Panzerwaffe* in some areas of the front. Once more, despite the setbacks, there was a genuine feeling of motivation within the ranks of the *Panzerwaffe*. There was renewed determination to keep the 'Red menace' out of the Homeland. In addition, confidence was further bolstered by the efforts of the armaments industry as they began producing many new vehicles for the Eastern Front. In fact, during 1944 the *Panzerwaffe* were better supplied with equipment during any other time on the Eastern Front thanks to the armaments industry. In total some 20,000 fighting vehicles including: 6,000 half-tracks of all variants, 8,328 medium and heavy tanks, 5,751 assault guns, 3,617 tank destroyers and 1,246 self-propelled artillery carriages of various types reached the Eastern Front. All of these vehicles would have to be irrevocably stretched along a very thin Eastern Front, with many of them rarely reaching the proper operating level. Panzer divisions too were often broken up and split among hastily constructed battle groups or *Kampfgruppe*, drawn from a motley collection of armoured formations. But still these battle groups were put into the line operating well below strength. The demands that were put upon the *Panzerwaffe* during the spring and summer of 1944 were immeasurable. The constant employment, coupled with the nightmare of not having enough supplies, was a worry that perpetually festered in the minds of the commanders. The Red

Army, encouraged by the Germans dire situation, was now mounting bolder operations aimed directly against the German front.

With renewed confidence Soviet commanders began drawing up plans for a massive concentration of forces along the entire frontline in central Russia. The new summer offensive was to be called 'Operation *Bagration*' and its objective was to annihilate Army Group Centre.

On the morning of 22 June, the third anniversary of the Soviet invasion, Operation *Bagration* was launched against Army Group Centre. The three German armies opposing them had thirty-seven divisions, weakly supported by armour, against 166 divisions, supported by 2,700 tanks and 1,300 assault guns. At the end of the first week of *Bagration* the three German armies had lost, between them, nearly 200,000 men and 900 tanks; 9th Army and the 3rd Panzer Army were almost decimated. The remnants of the shattered armies trudged back west in order to try and rest and refit what was left of its Panzer units and build new defensive lines. Any plans to regain the initiative on the Eastern Front were doomed forever.

With the complete obliteration of Army Group Centre, the Germans were even more hard pressed to contain their enemy. What followed during the last weeks of July was a frantic attempt by the *Panzerwaffe* to stem the rout of the Soviet drive into Poland. Army Group North Ukraine tried its best to contain its slender position on the River Bug, whilst remnants of Army Group Centre tied with all available resources to create a solid front line at Kaunas, Bialystok-Brest and assemble what was left of its forces on both its flanks. But between Army Group Centre and Army Group North, German positions were depleted.

Between June and September 1944, the Germans had sustained some 1,000,000 casualties. To make good their losses many of the exhausted and undermanned divisions were conscripted of old men and low-grade troops. The method of recruitment generally did not produce very good results. Not only were the number of recruits simply insufficient, but the enlistment of volunteers into the German Army was beginning to show signs of strain and exhaustion. In the *Panzerwaffe* too many of the replacement crews did not have sufficient time to be properly trained and, as a result, losses soared. Lack of fuel and not enough spare parts, coupled with the lack of trained crews all played a major part in reducing the effectiveness of the *Panzerwaffe* in the final year of the war. Yet despite this deficiency in men and equipment, the German Army did manage to slow down the Russian drive in the East, if only temporarily. On the central sector of the Eastern Front the remnants of the once vaunted Army Group Centre had steadily withdrawn across the Polish border westwards in July 1944.

However, just seven weeks later in September 1944, the whole position in Poland was on the point of disintegration. Action in Poland had been a grueling battle of attrition for those German units that had managed to escape from the slaughter.

Fortunately for the surviving German forces, the Soviet offensive had now run out of momentum. The Red Army's troops were too exhausted, and their armoured vehicles were in great need of maintenance and repair. Although it seemed the Germans had been spared from being driven out of Poland for the time being, their position in the East was on the verge of collapse. On 1 September, the Soviets had reached the Bulgarian border. Within a week, the Red Army reached the Yugoslav frontier. On 8 September, Bulgaria and Romania then declared war on Germany. Two weeks later on 23 September, Soviet forces arrived on the Hungarian border and immediately raced through the country for the Danube, finally reaching the river to the south of Budapest.

During the last months of 1944, the *Panzerwaffe* continued to try its utmost to contain its growing enemy. Drastic attempts by the Germans to improvise and up-gun their vehicles, including their half-tracks, did nothing to alter the situation. Slowly and systematically, the *Panzerwaffe* were ground down in a war of attrition.

FlaK gunners with their shielded 20mm *Flakvierling* 38. These quadruple-barrelled self-propelled anti-aircraft guns demonstrated outstanding anti-aircraft capabilities, even during the last months of the war. By this period of operations in the east, many of these weapons were being used against Russian heavy armour, which was also very effective.

A Sd.Kfz.6 from the Bulgarian Army can be seen advancing up a gradient. Note the registration plate with the letter 'B', which is followed by a five-digit number. This indicates that the vehicle is attached to the Bulgarian 1st Armoured Brigade.

A gunner with his mounted 37mm FlaK gun on an Sd.Kfz.10. These deadly guns were much respected by low-flying Russian airmen and were also particularly devastating against light vehicles, as well as troops caught in the open. The weapon also armed a variety of vehicles on self-propelled mounts where they could be moved from one part of the defensive line to another quickly and efficiently.

Sd.Kfz.251 half-tracks move across a field. Throughout the war on the Eastern Front the supply situation was exacerbated by the almost non-existence of proper roads throughout the Soviet Union. Half-tracks and other tracked vehicles were utilized to help speed up the supply of ammunition and other equipment desperately required for the front.

A half-track races along a road passing a burning building, which has evidently been set on fire by a 'Scorched Earth Policy'. During the German withdrawal from the East many thousands of buildings and important installations were set on fire in a drastic attempt to deny the enemy shelter or supplies.

General Model seen here standing next to a Sd.Kfz.251 in Poland in 1944. Many commanders in the field including the soldiers looked upon Model as the Führer's troubleshooter. It was Model that ordered his 'Shield and Sword' policy, which stated that retreats were tolerable, but only if they paved the way for a counterstroke later. Out on the battlefield Model was not only energetic, courageous and innovative, but was friendly and popular with his enlisted men.

A Sd.Kfz.251/3 advances along a road with two vehicles following closely behind. The *Panzerwaffe* continued to rigidly commit everything it still had. Despite the dogged resistance of many of the tank crews and supporting troops, there was no coherent strategy, and any local counter-offensives were often blunted with severe losses. The Soviets possessed too many tanks, anti-tank guns and aircraft for the Panzers and they remained incapable of causing any serious losses or delay.

Parked in some undergrowth is a *Panzerwerfer* prepared for a fire mission. This version was designated as the Sd.Kfz.4/1 and consisted of an armoured *Maultier* body with a ten-shot 15cm *Nebelwerfer* 42 rocket launcher mounted on the roof.

A FlaK gunner scans the sky through a pair of 6 × 30 field binoculars. He is standing next to a well camouflaged, shielded 20mm *Flakvierling* 38 quadruple-barrelled self-propelled anti-aircraft gun, which can be seen in an elevated position.

An SS FlaK gunner surveys the terrain ahead whilst standing onboard a Sd.Kfz.10/4 with a mounted shielded 20mm *Flakvierling* 38. Foliage has been applied to the splinter shield in order to try and break-up the distinctive shape of the gun.

A number of Sd.kfz.251 in a field during intensive heavy fighting. The Sd.Kfz.251 had become not just a half-track intended to simply transport infantry to the edge of the battlefield, but also a fully-fledged fighting vehicle.

A Sd.Kfz.251 armoured personnel carrier can be seen moving along a road. Halted at the side of the road is a late variant Pz.Kpfw.IV with intact side skirts. By late 1944, there was little in the way of reinforcements reaching German units in the field, and those that were left holding a defensive position had already been forced into various *ad hoc* Panzer divisions that were simply thrown together with a handful of tanks and *Panzergrenadiers*. Much of these hastily formed formations were short-lived. The majority were either completely decimated in the fighting or had received such a mauling in battle they were reorganized into a different *ad hoc* formation under a new commander.

Two Sd.Kfz.251 armoured personnel carriers have halted on a road with well armed *Panzergrenadiers* ready at a moment's notice to dismount. For the troops this was the most effective and quickest way of being transported either to the battlefield, or being withdrawn to another line of defence. When the half-tracks arrived at the edge of a battlefield, the troops were able to quickly dismount to take up positions.

A Sd.Kfz.11 hauls a 105mm artillery piece along a dusty road. Note the divisional insignia painted in yellow on the rear of the half-track. This indicates that the half-track is attached to the SS-Division *'Wiking'*.

Panzergrenadiers on the march in 1944. A stationary Sd.Kfz.250 can be seen which still retains its winter whitewash camouflage paint. For the *Panzerwaffe* fighting for survival on the Eastern Front, shortages of every kind were affecting most of the old and experienced Panzer divisions. The Soviets had unmatchable material superiority. Yet, despite this major drawback in late 1944, armoured vehicle production, including half-tracks, tanks, assault guns, and self-propelled assault guns, was higher than in any month before May 1944. In October and November 1944, assembly plants managed to turn out 12,000 trucks by rebuilding disabled vehicles and transporting them both to the Eastern and Western Fronts.

In Poland and a Sd.Kfz.7 crosses a waterlogged field following a torrential down-pour. The vehicle has a coating of winter whitewash paint. By September 1944, the whole position in Poland was on the point of disintegration. Action in Poland had been a grueling battle of attrition for those German units that had managed to escape from the slaughter.

During winter operations in Poland and *Waffen-SS* troops can be seen hitching a lift on board a Sd.Kfz.10/4. The half-track mounts a shielded 20mm FlaK 30 gun and tows a S.Ah.51 trailer.

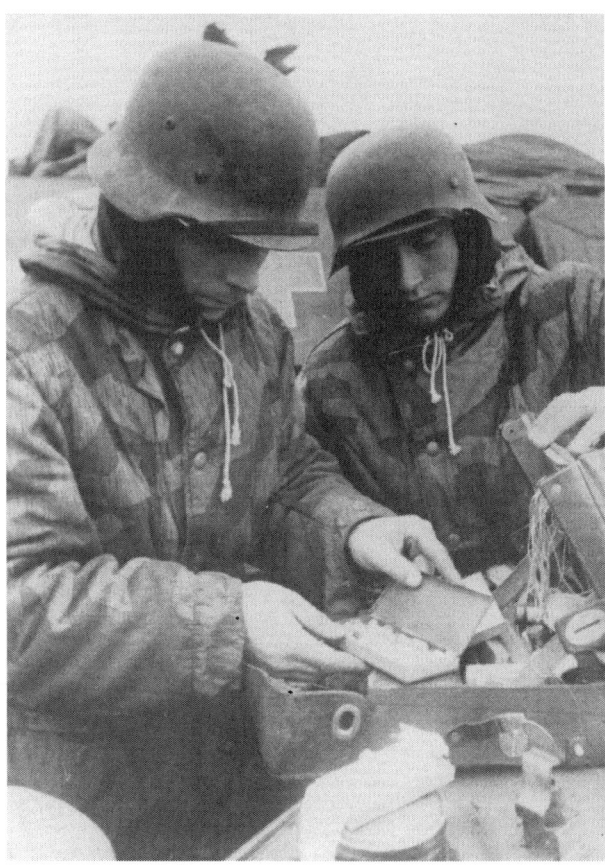 

Two photographs taken in sequence showing a medic tending to an injured comrade next to a Sd.Kfz.251. All of the troops wear the green splinter pattern, army camouflage smocks. These smocks were very popular among the *Wehrmacht* and proved to be an extremely comfortable combat garment, giving the wearer plenty of movement and freedom and, at the same time, plenty of concealment.

A Sd.Kfz.251 armoured personnel carrier appears to be towing a truck across a river during winter operations in Poland in 1944. Despite fervent efforts to increase the combat strength of the *Panzerwaffe*, Panzer units and individuals of Panzer and *Panzergrenadier* divisions were too exhausted to avert the situation decisively. As a result, the Russians continued pushing forward, whilst German forces retreated through Poland to East Prussia.

Two Sd.Kfz.251, one an Ausf.C and the other an Ausf.D, pull alongside each other during winter operations in Russia. The crew appear to be exchanging details. The Ausf.C mounts the typical frame antenna, while the Ausf.D has no antenna. Both mount the MG34 machine gun with splinter shield.

Here a crewman prepares to launch his *Panzerwerfer*. He is standing on the open hatches, through which rockets are being passed. Note a jerrycan wedged behind the forward wheels to help keep the vehicle from moving when the rockets were fired. The back blast from the *Nebelwerfer* was very powerful and could often move a vehicle as large as this by a foot.

This *Panzerwerfer* can be seen racing through the snow towards the battlefront. Note the MG34 has been mounted on the driver's compartment roof for local defence.

Chapter Six

1945

On 12 January 1945, the Eastern Front erupted with a massive advance as Konev's offensive began with the 1st Ukrainian Front, making deep wide-sweeping penetrations against hard-pressed German formations. The Russian offensive was delivered with so much weight and fury, never before experienced on the Eastern Front. The Russians had total numerical superiority over the Germans with seven to one in armour alone. The vast tide of the Red Army soon swallowed up the battlefield and, by the end of the first day of the new offensive, it had torn a huge breach over 20 miles wide in the Vistula front.

On 14 January, Zhukov's 1st Belorrussian Front began its long awaited drive along the Warsaw–Berlin Axis, striking out from the Vistula south of Warsaw. The city was quickly encircled and fell three days later. The frozen ground ensured rapid movement for the Russian tank crews, but in some areas these massive advances were halted for a time by the skilful dispositions of the *Panzerwaffe*. Determinedly they held out in small groups of grenadiers supported by Panzers, until they too were annihilated or forced to fall back.

By 25 January, the Russians stood in front of Breslau and two days later the city of Memel fell. As German forces continued to fall back, they tried frantically to prevent the Red Army from bursting across the borders of the Reich and onto the River Oder, which was no more than 50 miles from the Reich capital, Berlin.

Along 200 miles of the defensive front the remaining Panzer divisions had no more than seventy tanks strung out along the front lines and were almost totally unprotected. In spite the overwhelming superiority, German forces prepared their defensive positions along the Oder. However, both the *Wehrmacht* and their *Waffen-SS* counterparts had neither the manpower, war plants or transportation to accomplish a proper build-up of forces on the Oder. Commanders could do little to compensate for the deficiencies, and in many sectors of the front they did not have any coherent planning in the event that the defence of the river failed. When the Russians successfully attacked the Oder in mid-April 1945, the hodgepodge force of what was left of the German Army fought out in desperation as the Soviet thrust carved its way across the river, capturing the town of Kustrin, and heading towards the Nazi capital.

A Sd.Kfz.251 armoured personnel carrier pulls alongside a Sd.Kfz.10/4 on a road somewhere in eastern Germany. The crew of both vehicles have applied extensive foliage over the half-tracks. By the latter half of the war it had become very dangerous for armoured crews to travel by road during daylight hours.

Waffen-SS troops can be seen standing next to their FlaK gun during a lull in the defensive fighting. In the foreground two Sd.Kfz.10/4 half-tracks can be seen moving along a road flanking a Sd.Kfz.7, towing what appears to be a 150mm s.IG33 howitzer.

Here in the snow preparing for a fire mission are a number of *Panzerwerfer* and ammunition wagons. Note the discarded gun tube packages in a heap in the snow. These have been loaded through the vehicle hatches from the wagons in readiness for firing.

A Sd.Kfz.7 towing an 88mm FlaK 36 or 37 passes a halted *Panzerjäger* Tiger (P) 'Ferdinand'. Both vehicles have interesting camouflage schemes comprising of a web type patter effect, which has been created by spraying a lighter colour over the dark sand base colour.

A rare photograph showing a specially converted half-track with a mounted 37mm FlaK 37 in its elevated position during winter operations. Note the gunner gazing through the tripod-mounted binoculars, trying to deduce the whereabouts of enemy aerial activity.

A column of Sd.Kfz.251 half-tracks belonging to an unidentified *Waffen-SS* unit can be seen moving along a road. These vehicles were used extensively during the latter half of the war to transport *Panzergrenadiers* to the forward edge of the battlefield. Despite being lightly armoured, they could maintain a relatively modest speed and manoeuvre across country and keep up with the fast-moving spearheads.

Halted next to a lake in Hungary is a line of Sd.Kfz.251/1 Ausf.D. They are all well camouflaged and are painted in a base colour of dark yellow with over sprayed patches and zig-zags of olive green, red and brown.

A photograph taken the moment a battery of *Maultiers* open fire against an enemy target during defensive fighting in the latter stages of the war. The last great offensive that brought the Russians their final victory in the East began during the third week of January 1945. The principal objective was to crush the remaining German forces in Poland, East Prussia and the Baltic states.

An officer converses with a Sd.Kfz.251 crew member during a lull in the fighting during the final months of the war. During these last months it seemed the Germans were being constantly forced to retreat. Many isolated units spent hours or even days fighting a bloody defence.

Along a typical German defensive position in the latter stages of the war. Here *Wehrmacht* troops have dug-in and are being defended by armour. In the foreground Sd.Kfz.251 armoured personnel carriers can be seen moving across a field.

A *Waffen-SS* Sd.Kfz.10/4 mounting a shielded 20mm FlaK gun attempts to cross a river. Alongside the half-track a truck appears to be experiencing some kind of difficulty in the icy water.

A Sd.Kfz.10 hauling a FlaK gun along a typical muddy road during a defensive withdrawal in the last months of the war. The vehicle is following a horse drawn cart. During the last months of the war, as fuel supplies diminished and losses in armour soared, animal draught became the most predominant way of travelling from one part of the receding front to another.

On a very muddy road a VW *Kübelwagen* has halted next to a half-track. Two soldiers are seen conversing. The bad road system in the East had been a constant problem to the German Army throughout the war. As a result of many of the roads being turned into a quagmire, German defensive and offensive operations were often severely affected.

A Sd.Kfz.10 drives slowly along a very muddy road, more than likely to a medical facility at the rear. By the type of winter uniforms being worn by these soldiers they are attached to a *Waffen-SS* unit.

The last battles being fought in front of Berlin and here a pair of *Panzergrenadiers*, each armed with the *Panzerfaust* 30, stand next to a camouflaged Sd.Kfz.251 armoured personnel carrier.

Appendix

Artillery Prime Movers

Sd.Kfz.2   Sd.Kfz.8   Sd.Kfz.10   Maultier
Sd.Kfz.7   Sd.Kfz.9   Sd.Kfz.11

Variants of the Sd.Kfz.251

251/1a Schützen Panzer Wg
Versions: Ausf ABCD
Carried ten riflemen and all their equipment, plus a two-man crew consisting of a driver and commander. Two MG34s were fitted.

251/1b Schützen Panzer Wg
Versions: Ausf ABC
Carried nine fully equipped riflemen and a heavy mount for the MG34.

251 Schütz Panzer Wg Wurfrahmen
Versions: Ausf ABCD
Mounted of launch crates containing 'Wurfrahmen' rockets. Six of these heavy 280mm HE or 320mm napalm rocket launched projectiles could be carried. The rockets were launched with the crew outside the vehicle.

251/2 Schütz Panzer Wg Granatenwurfer
Versions: Ausf CD
Introduced in early 1941 and carried an 80mm mortar. The mortar could be fired both from inside the vehicle or dismounted outside on a ground plate carried on the superstructure.

251/3 Funk Panzer Wg
Versions: Ausf CD
Designed primarily for light ordnance such as the 37mm PaK 36, 50mm PaK 38, 75mm PaK 40 and the heavier infantry gun the 105mm leFH 18. In early 1943, the 251/3 reverted to a communications role.

251/6 Kommand Panzer Wg
Versions: Ausf ABCD
A commanders vehicle, later equipped with various decoding and deciphering apparatus and a variety of radios and antenna.

251/7 Pioneer Panzer Wg
Versions: Ausf CD
To provide transportation for various engineer sections and their equipment.

251/8 Krankenpanzerwagen
Versions: Ausf BCD
An armoured ambulance which could carry two stretchers and four seated wounded. Later models had redesigned doors to allow for easy entry and exit.

251/9 Schütz Panzer Wg 75mm K Kanonenwagen
Versions: Ausf CD
Fitted with a forward-firing 75mm KwK 37 L/24 gun and was used to provide armoured reconnaissance units with fire support.

251/10 Schütz Panzer Wg 37mm Pak
Versions: Ausf ABCD
Primarily designed to carry the 37mm PaK 36 which was fitted on top of the armour above the driver and co-driver. Later, a mounting for the gun and an armoured shield were fitted.

251/11 Fernsprech Panzer Wg
Versions: Ausf C
Served as an armoured cable-laying vehicle.

251/12 Messtr u Geräte Panzer Wg
Versions: Ausf BC
Introduced as an artillery survey section vehicle which specialized in artillery observation.

251/13 Schallaufn Panzer Wg
Versions: Ausf C
Equipped with instruments to record and examine the sound of enemy artillery batteries and then locate their position.

251/14 Schallausw Panzer Wg
Versions: Ausf C
Equipped with specialized sound ranging instruments to interpret the sound of enemy artillery and then locate their position.

251/15 Lichtausw Panzer Wg
Versions: Ausf C
Equipped with flash spotting instruments to interpret the flashes of enemy artillery and then locate their position.

251/16 Mittlerer Flammpanzerwagen
Versions: Ausf CD
Fitted with two 14mm Flammenwerfer, one on each side of the superstructure, which were fitted with armoured shields.

251/17 Mittlerer Schützenpanzerwagen (20mm) Flak
Fitted with either a 20mm Flak 30 or Flak 38. Designed primarily for anti-aircraft protection.

251/18 Mittlerer Beobachtungspanzerwagen
Versions: Ausf CD
Used as a mobile observation post and command vehicle, replacing the 251/6.

251/19 Mittlerer Fernsprech-Betriebspanzerwagen
Versions: Ausf D
Served as an armoured telephone relay unit.

251/22 Mittleren Schützenpanzerwagen 75mm Pak 40
Versions: Ausf D
Introduced to carry the 75mm Pak 40.

Variants of the light Sd.Kfz.250

Sd.Kfz.250/1 Schützenpanzerwagen
Introduced for various reconnaissance tasks. It was also used as a platoon and company commander's vehicle. The command vehicle was equipped with various decoding and deciphering apparatus and a variety of radios and antenna.

Sd.Kfz.250/2 Fernsprechpanzerwagen
Entered service as an armored telephone cable layer and was also used as an observation vehicle. The vehicle could lay up to three cables at a time.

Sd.Kfz.250/3 Funkpanzerwagen
This vehicle was a communications vehicle and was fitted with a variety of radios and antenna.

Sd.Kfz.250/4 Truppenluftschützpanzerwagen
This vehicle was an air liason and observation vehicle and was used by *Luftwaffe* forward air controllers to contact aircraft and guide them onto their targets.

Sd.Kfz.250/5 Beobachtungspanzerwagen
This vehicle was a forward observation vehicle for assault gun batteries.

Sd.Kfz.250/6 Munitionspanzerwagen
This vehicle served as an ammunition carrier for assault guns. The vehicle could be fitted internally to carry either seventy rounds for the short 75mm StuK 37 L/24 gun or sixty rounds for the long 75mm StuK 40 L/43 gun.

Sd.Kfz.250/7 Schützenpanzerwagen schwerer Granatwerfer
This vehicle was adapted to carry the 80mm mortar.

Sd.Kfz.250/8 Schützenpanzerwagen 75mm
Fitted with a forward firing 75mm KwK 37 L/24 gun. It was used to provide armored reconnaissance units with integral fire support.

Sd.Kfz.250/9 Schützenpanzerwagen 20mm
Built primarily to replace the wheeled armored cars, which were unsuitable for the terrain conditions in Russia. The turret assembly of the Sd.Kfz.222 was fitted on to the top of the superstructure, which was roofed to accommodate it.

Sd.Kfz.250/10 Schützenpanzerwagen 37mm PaK
Built with the standard 37mm PaK 36 fitted on top of the armor above the driver and co-driver. Later, a mounting for the gun and an armored shield were fitted.

Sd.Kfz.250/11 Schützenpanzerwagen schwere Panzerbüchse
This vehicle replaced the Sd.Kkfz.250/10 as the platoon commanders vehicle.

Sd.Kfz.250/12 Messtruppanzerwagen
This vehicle was built to replace the Sd.Kfz.251/13. It was used as an artillery survey and observation vehicle.

The Publisher's authorised representative in the EU for product safety is Authorised Rep Compliance Ltd, Ground Floor, 71 Lower Bagot St, Dublin, Ireland, D02 P593 www.arccompliance.com

Printed and bound by CPI Group (UK) Ltd, Croydon, CR0 4YY
20/03/2026
02075728-0001